INCOHERENT RAMBLINGS OF THE DAMNED

PAIGE PENNINGTON

authorHOUSE®

AuthorHouse™ UK
1663 Liberty Drive
Bloomington, IN 47403 USA
www.authorhouse.co.uk
Phone: UK TFN: 0800 0148641 (Toll Free inside the UK)
      UK Local: (02) 0369 56322 (+44 20 3695 6322 from outside the UK)

Published by AuthorHouse 10/27/2023

ISBN: 979-8-8230-8523-6 (sc)
ISBN: 979-8-8230-8522-9 (e)

Library of Congress Control Number: 2023919861

Print information available on the last page.

Any people depicted in stock imagery provided by Getty Images are models,
and such images are being used for illustrative purposes only.
Certain stock imagery © Getty Images.

This book is printed on acid-free paper.

Just like jam that has been slapped onto two slices of bread, I find myself with an indescribable hunger for more.

Let us not squabble like siblings, let us be close like friends.

Many find my ramblings torture, but they do not know the torture that it is to be me.

To be as I have been let and to be with a turmoil none but I can grasp.

Please hear my plea as I say:

Let it be gone! Let it be gone! Let it be gone!

"You unfortunate fool."

"I care not what they think," I say, even though it is untrue.

The truth is grim and can leave me inconsolable for days.

Oh, the end!

How merciful it would be to me if only I knew how to get there.

I have the means but not the knowledge, and for that, I curse the very being who thought it wise to put me here.

I will not be merciful in my revenge, as I will not stop until I can serve its head on a silver platter for all to see.

I fear my mother has begun to resent me,

Me and my mouth,

Me and my problems,

How could she not when it is so easy to hate and so hard to love?

I fear I could not love my children unconditionally because I have
seen firsthand how hard it is to do that.

My mother is my rock, an immovable force in my life, and yet she
undoubtedly hates me.

Do not feel bad if you are hated because you are simply
misunderstood in a place where no one cares for anything
beyond the tip of their nose.
While I am too entrapped in the confines of my mind.
No matter what I say, that's untrue.
All I wish is to matter as much as others matter to me.
I wish to stand on the pedestal, proud and in the first place.

I want to feel it.

I want to see it,

Trickling down and pooling onto the floor.

I hate that I feel the need for it, yet I do anyway.

Desperate for any kind of release.

A kind of release that none but you can fulfill, my sweet, come
    to me.

Let us play our melody one last time.

I've noticed that I am staring at walls an increasing amount,
lost in a blank stare, dozing in and out of self-awareness.
I am rapidly losing my whole sense of self, lost in the war that
    seems to be constantly raging in the makings of my mind,
and I can barely make heads or tails in the midst of it all.

A storm is brewing, but not just in me. It's inside everybody, everywhere, fighting for sense. I am lost among the lost. "Ye of little faith," they say. Well, I say pity the fool who is sane in a world of the insane.

The insane get me as they have seen the darkest corners of my mind and simply nod their acknowledgment to share their own beastly side.

Beasts who eat other beasts will survive, while those living off the land will perish - perish they will as the old maid said, "perish to ash as lumber they were."

Why am I desensitized by such ghastly beings? Because beneath the fur, claws, and teeth is but a child - simply pleading to be freed from their inner nightmare of a world.

They shout and cry out, "How dare I be me?
Well, how dare you be you?
At least when I am me, I do it in an unabashed way, stumbling
    and bumbling yet - still kind.
When you are you, you are simply cruel.
Cruel like the harsh winds on a winter morning,
Leaving my cheeks red-raw and tears brimming in my eyes.
I told you, no more!
But then again, when did you ever listen?

Simple acts of service
And sweet little "love-you-so's"
Trickling into my ears like rain at summer morn
Cool yet warm and kind - like you
Oh, I love you so!
As if you were the moon and me the sun.
So it be as I want it to be, at least for a little while.

Oh, how she calls to me,
Like a sweet mistress
Waiting for me even though she is not the one I have home
Oh, how she lulls me with her melodic moans of pleasure
I just want her to be with me all the time, day and night.
But it is not what we have fated
Even if, under oath we never truly were, I will keep you there, in
    our summer of rendezvous.

I'm a jealous person. Not openly, well, not always openly.
I let it sit and sink into the roots of my brain and let it feast on
   my very being.
Feast it does until I am a withered, grumpy little hag.

Shooting down an open road
Not quite safe from myself
But also not quite safe from the fact that life is how it is
and I have no say in the matter.

Hate me as I hate me,
Hate me as I wish to be hated.
It is a thing none but I have dared ask you to do.
I stunned you.
And yet, here we are -
So full of hate for one another but still there in times like these.

It's not war, but it's close - it's grief, and it kills you from the inside
out, starting with your sweet memories and turning them sour.

It makes you mad — an inescapable madness that never ends
because you're not here anymore. I wish you were here. I wish
and I wish until my cheeks are red and my tongue is numb.
But no amount of wishing can undo what has been done. It's
a cruel lesson, and it's one that you learn too many times.

It kills me to admit it, but we are nothing but defenseless prey.
Like lambs laid to slaughter for some higher reason that I do
not care to understand because I am blinded by my grief.

I'm just trying to dig myself out of the quicksand, scrambling but
sinking, trying to move an immovable force.

How dare they take you when there was so much more that you
had left to do? It's not "bittersweet," it's poisonous, and I'm
sick of pretending that it's not.

It is a thing that has me walking around with my hands as my feet, and my feet as my hands.

It's a complicated force of being constantly put against one another,

But how dare we all cause them to fight when they wish nothing but the best of us?

It is a ludicrous thing and no matter how many times they seem to disagree - they are just playing as you wished them to.

There is no malice behind their words and not enough conviction for us to believe them,

And yet we choose the harder path anyway and choose to believe their harsh words - because what is a world without hate?

In a world where you aren't you and I'm not me -
Do you think we could have been meant to be?
Lost and unmoving
In love, so hopelessly in love.
Oh, how I wish with all of me how it could be our reality,
But here I am, with me being me and you being you with our
tragic fate of never meant to be.

Sometimes, I think about jumping off of a bridge,
Into cool water -
Just to feel something other than the constant ache.
Sometimes, I think about stepping into speeding traffic -
Just to see if someone would notice.
Sometimes I think that, I am too much to deal with.
No, always I know, I am too much to deal with,
But try as I might -
I just can not stop myself from the haunting that is the way I am.

Give a man power and he will go mad trying not to lose it
But withhold power from a man and he will go mad searching
for it.
I have never had power.
But you did and you abused it - you abused me.
And what didn't show up in scars and bruises,
Showed up in tear-stained cheeks and a broken shell of the
woman I used to be.

Why give a gift if you are just going to take it away?
What higher being decided this?
"Life is a gift."
Until it is a curse.
Everyone goes eventually, whether we want too or not.
I just hope that wherever "there" is, you are content and we will
    meet again someday.

It's on days like this that I am filled with an incomparable bliss,
One that leaves a soft humming in my head,
Like bees on a summers day - except it's in tune to your secret
    melody and I find myself dancing along with them.
Content with the fact that you would be proud of me for simply
    finding myself again, and so unapologetically so!

I'm like a ticking clock, a bomb that is about to go off.
Tick, tick, tick.
Musn't be harsh.
Must be kind.
Cannot snap.
Must smile.
Must behave
Must give time.
Tick, tick, tick.
This clock is killing me!
I must be sensitive, to the problem of my head.
Uncovering the quiet voice call's in me.
Tick, tick, tick.
No!

Everyone is trying to save me,
Unluckily for them - the darkness is my one true inspiration and I
    would prefer to drown in it than to be lost without it.
My madness is my being and no-one can convince me otherwise.

If I could portal us back to that place again, I would.
Without a single doubt in my mind, I would.
In a world that we created in our innocent, childish minds.
That I stayed in.
Instead of the real, cruel world that we were born into.
That you are now in.
I stay here in the hopes of you returning to me one day, back
   into our perfect, make-believe land.
Safe from outsiders and outside problems.

I need to feel carefree again and to remove the weight of being
me from my shoulders.
I have been noticing cracks in my reality for quite some time and
I have been choosing to ignore them,
They were small at first -
Shadow-beings in my peripheral vision and bugs crawling on me
and waking me from my slumber.
But they are too large to ignore now,
Because you had three heads last time that we met.

I never, ever wish to harm anyone, ever.

Yet, here I am.

In an aftermath of a problem that I supposedly made and everyone involved are more than happy to pin whatever even happened on me.

Everyone is looking at me and I'm not sure if I am supposed to speak, or move, or just break down.

But the truth is I have nothing to say and I want to say something.

At least, I want to apologise for the trouble I have caused.

But I can't find the words.

Trapped in a situation that is portrayed as "ideal"
But as I watch the flames lick at his face, I feel a surge of dread
that there's Nothing he can do to stop this from happening.
And a visceral sadness that he has to be involved in something
that might not have actually been his fault, but is the sad
legacy of a family who do not love as they should.

How tragic that there will always be darkness.
And how sweetly right, even in the darkest moments, the sun
     breaks through.
For the young man I loved,
I held him as he died, and that was the end of my love for him.
But the memories of a boy who never grew old,
Are with me still.
So sweet and so sad,
Love outlives death,
And the memory of the heart I loved,
Is as golden as the leaves of autumn.

Sunshine, warm, morning kiss
Dreams in full colour, eyes raked by the boughs
Even the night do not hide
The night's look, as daylight looks on white feathers,
White feathers from the overripe peach tree, white
Weeping willows, when they open on my boots, white
Blue maple, swaying in the wind, lifting the broken tops
Into the sky, candle-bright in the sunset, looking almost pink, in
    my face
Sunflower leaves, full of light, with just a hint of yellow, the seeds
    still there,
sudden shock of yellow, white blossoms opening, then, snow, like
    bits of leaf floating on a sea of light

you roll along
clutching this and that
curled up in a ball
losing control
breaking down
yet again

True love isn't something we acquire or develop. It's an inward
thing: it is born in us in moments of intimacy with another, it
is fashioned by us in moments of courage, and it is nurtured
by us in moments of love and generosity.

First, I wanted to make sure that I wasn't wrong.

I wanted to make sure that this didn't just seem like a well-
considered, heartfelt thought, written with lightening speed
and exquisite clarity.

I wanted to make sure that he was in a good place with himself,
that he hadn't, through being distracted, stopped, and instead
built a wall around himself, made of withering sentences and
soaring heights of evanescent inspiration, so huge and strong
that it may as well be of red brick and concrete.

I wanted to make sure that it wasn't simply so clever a way of
grabbing the attention of readers, and that he was actually,
at the core of his being, a person who listened to what
people said and understood it

and now, you say, and so I said, that I was wrong.

you weren't wrong.

The rumbling of the heavens
And the quaking of his soul
Retreating deeper into the night's secret folds
Before the dawn can break upon him
Bringing with it more pain,
And questions, and worries
The unbearable curiosity,
The will to answer
The melody

Between myself and you
So must I be, as I feel that it is time.
People going, hither, on, every way at speed,
Flowing, looking into the cracks of the rocks,
As if looking for some dark matter that cannot be
Observed, but cannot find, our fascination,
The question of us - how we are made
what is,
why, where,
And if there is a purpose,
or meaning - beyond what can be explained,
in any language,
As we may find it.

Fly from cliff to cliff
Have tails like a pendulum,
curl the wings down,
Look like stars
and don't
They swim through the sea
creeping down the stream
seeping into the stone
the cells in the bones.

I can't take it back.

I cannot take the feeling when I watch the grass grow and the
air turn green and move in a breeze, and you ask me if the
sound of a bird in the trees

is like the sound of a bird in the sky.

And when you look at the sun and see the stars,

The way the trees and the water's blue.

How have I grown so much older?

You know, the way you die, when a finger stops working?

I don't think about the time that has passed.

I can't.

I can't believe it.

Times frozen, I'm trapped in an alternate reality.

I've lost more than I know, and I wonder how long I've been asleep and dreaming, and when I will wake up to life as it once was.

Waking, breathing, seeing.

I'm dying, and I don't know why.

The darkness chokes me.

I try to claw my way out, but I don't move.

My mouth opens, and my words disappear.

The lights and the warmth of all is gone
Night is so dark and grey, but something stirs through
The sleeping world of night
In his own quiet lonely way, waiting patiently for his moment,
That won't come.
How peaceful is it outside at night
With the heavy rain that
Folds over the land
Rain on a glass
Into a misty glass
But what is calm and still
Is beyond the black seas of doubt
The pulse of life,
The dark waters of sleep
The pangs of pain,
He lifts his head at his hiding place
And waits, looking, looking, into the deep dark recesses of his
    mind
So for now he makes his own sound.

Death.

The ultimate sacrifice. This once beautiful, amazing thing is now reduced to the unredeemable, grotesque beast of a thing you see before you.

An embodiment of a cycle we can never escape.

It's a cycle that will keep on repeating itself until it burns itself to ashes and remains nothing more than a memory.

It's a cycle that holds so much power over us and in the end, it is what makes us human.

It is what makes us vulnerable.

It is a cycle that sucks the life from everything we love, and turns it into death.

It never meant to exist.

It never wanted to be here.

It was an accident waiting to happen.

It's not here to cause us pain, it's not here to take our lives from us.

It's here to teach us lessons, and the lessons it has taught me have not been pleasant.

It's here to prove a point and remind us that life is precious and fleeting and every moment is the last.

I have been reborn again and again and again.

This one was the darkest and hardest to accept.

To grasp.

This one's teeth sunk deep into my heart.

It has changed my life.

I never thought anything could hurt this much.

But it did.

It did.

Why does the sun rise and set, and the morning, and the evening
   have fragrance?
I, who am without bound, with a gasp on every occasion breathe
   as if alive.
Everything is sweet, all things are on fire and thirst for me. Let me
   not speak of sweetness without a similar rapture.
The heat of me must be enough for those who, in their extremity,
   desire it. What has this radiant beauty? Take me! Take me!
Hark and listen! Dear and ever true.

So, what have the exuberant walls done to me, who breathe for them and pine for them, but to make them love me more?

Love me more than it loves!

I am the blood of those that love, but their love is love to the soul, which grows only from the blood of those who love me.

It is here that the body, with horror, needs to be healed, for it was made to be touched, tasted and loved.

The rib must be drawn through the finger, and thought with the tears of the heart.

Are you, not mine,

In a prison where all are imprisoned?

It is here where the head has a truth that cannot be explained to the mind, where the tongue is given power to speak freely, and where the mouth is so full of the joy of those who love that it needs no other voice to express the love.

It is here, in this little house, where the hand is lonely and has only me to touch, where the mouth trembles and becomes the proof of the soul, where the skin is driven back by the thorn of life, and where the heart, where the bones ache for the touch of those that love, and who are loved by those that love.

In my heart, in my thoughts, in my lips, and in my eyes,
I am more lovely than that which is born.
Take me and give me your heart,
Your gentle and easily forgotten kindness,
Your quiet love and your ever-before-falling grace.
Lovers lay your hair on the brow of your head.

Hear, O ears, the moan of the hand, and of the heart; let it be
   still and silent.
It is here that the flower, more than those of the arms,
Should have a fragrance for the heart and a fragrance that is
   more than the perfume.
It is here that the wood waits to grow, and here, after nightfall,
   when the stars are dispersed and the moon sets, let the
   woodland grasses grow.

Your hands were made for shaking, not for speaking,but to the
    heart, I am always your mouth and you are always my eyes,
Vain are your eyes, weak are your hands,
Let them be directed to the soul and not to the body.

The leaves wave an inevitable farewell and in our hearts they say, goodbye to innocence.

After they've gone and the next wave moves in, reclaiming the beach with its shiny debris, having grabbed our imagination with its memory, our mind looks for another fresh memory to entertain us.

We hear the stillness of autumn, we watch the tree in the corner of the yard, and it turns out we are the only ones left.

and there's a reason for that, the quiet sets in, and the soft shush of leaves settling in, concludes the day.

At first, as I write these words, I'm struck with the solitude of it all, and the sense of it, the air as it disperses through my lungs, and so I look down and I watch the leaves.

And like the thoughts that wander through the forest to me, the leaves have a story to tell, which they've already told, and they want to tell it again.

But we won't let them, they're already gone, and we aren't, and this time they say, let me show you, let me show you.

And they continue their journey finding their way out of the woods, there's a gate in the fence and they must get through.

and so they scatter away,

Delivering on its promise of quietly taking you by surprise... but only a promise in a field with a thousand promises. Look for tricks at the level of sound and rhythm. A listener can find that trio of ushers slipping between them, one of whom is bearing a burden of words at his feet.

Whether reflecting the whims of the universe, or enmeshed in the human story, in the hands of someone like you.

If I knew who I was, I might choose to write things down that are
no longer true, and not see the difference. But I don't know.
The system is far too vast. Perhaps I should count the stars . . . but
I've been to places you can't imagine . . . there's no place to
hide, not any more.
I trust you. It's the only thing I can do.
Time. I've been waiting for you . . . for a long time.
Who will bring the light?
And all the while I've been gathering the bits of sky. Everything
falls away . . . The first place you took me, I don't recognize . . .
so far from the little stones, like the taste of forgetfulness.

So much change for a little girl like me
Not through fear, I hope.
A fickle carelessness or, perhaps, too much carelessness.
Oaths cannot take the blame
It will be the light you have brought me, only the brightness will
    burn, so I'll be careful to do what I must do.
We keep trying to tell ourselves we can't feel
It's simple. We think we're responsible but the heart might be
    nearer to the truth.
And I would like to believe you won't leave me alone in this place
But it's a lie I'm already alone and I don't want to wait any
    longer.
You might not realize I've been here before, just like you
Perhaps I've seen this song in a dream, or heard it on the wind.
    But it seems as fresh and pure as first time.

waking up feeling empty and not worth the cost.

it is knowing that every moment you lose just to find you have lost a little bit more.

it is knowing the physical pain that exists, and thinking it has nothing to do with the emotional pain.

it is giving your heart away, to give it back on the anniversary of when you last gave it away.

but this is nothing more than the web of our human existence.

the type of pain you feel in your neck at night, is the pain someone else has felt.

the pain that is felt in the hopelessness you feel, is the pain someone else has felt.

it is a pathway that leads to these moments.

where you can choose to run from the truth.

what you feel is not the truth.

because that truth is somewhere within you.

just buried.

but can you forgive the doubt that sits in your heart and tells you that you are never worthy to have that smile in the mirror?

that everything about you is wrong, and must be changed?

Printed in the United States
by Baker & Taylor Publisher Services